I0390504

The Compleat Apple iPhone® and iPad® Camera Guide

USEFUL TIPS THAT AREN'T IN THE MANUALS

Use the Hidden Capabilities of the iPhone 6s Plus, the iPhone 6s, the iPhone 6, the iPhone 5s, the iPad Pro, the iPad Air 2 & the iPad Air Cameras That Aren't Explained in the Manuals.

"Part of the Apple mystique is that they provide one of the world's most sophisticated cameras—without a manual."

-Anonymous

By
Steve Frankel

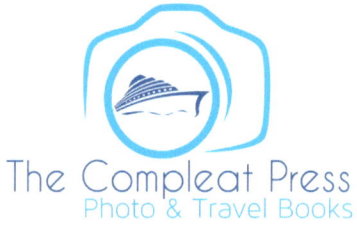

The Compleat Press
Playa del Rey, CA
www.TheCompleatPress.com

Publication Date: November 2015

Edited by Melissa Caminneci
Cover Designed by Ridha Yousaf
Cover Photo by Getty Images
Production by Lybomyr Yatsyk

IF YOU ENJOY THIS BOOK, PLEASE GIVE US A **LIKE** AT OUR FACEBOOK SITE, www.Facebook.com/TheCompleatPress, WHERE YOU'RE ALSO INVITED TO CONTRIBUTE YOUR FAVORITE iPHONE AND iPAD PHOTOS; AND PLEASE REGISTER AT OUR WEBSITE, www.TheCompleatPress.com FOR FREE UPDATES AND NEWS OF UPCOMING EVENTS AND BOOKS.

Table of Contents

Do You Need To Read This Book?

If you're like our typical reader, you've probably been using iPhone and iPad cameras for years. You probably think you're reasonably good with them! You may not be sure that you need this book—no matter how brief and informal it is.

Here is a Two-Minute True-or-False Quiz to predict whether this book will benefit you. Have fun and decide for yourself! Please cover up the right-hand column until you have answered all ten questions.

True or False

1. Except for screen size, the iPhone 6s and the iPhone 6s Plus have the same camera.	FALSE- The 6s Plus has Optical Image Stabilization (OIS) and a higher-resolution viewing screen.
2. The real name of the main iPhone 6s camera is the iSight.	TRUE- For some reason Apple doesn't use this name in many of their ads.
3. New iPhone cameras can take landscape photos that appear to be 3-dimensional.	TRUE- This feature is called HDR (High Dynamic Range).
4. There are a few meaningful differences between an iPhone 5s Camera and an iPad Air 2 Camera.	FALSE- There are no meaningful differences.
5. An iPhone 6s feature allows the camera to take a brief video clip automatically before and after every photo.	TRUE- This feature is called Live Photos.
6. The zoom range for most recent iPhones is from 35mm to 70mm.	FALSE- iPhones don't have zoom lenses.
7. The camera in the new iPad Pro technology is less advanced than the camera in the iPhone 6s.	TRUE- The camera in the iPad Pro has about the same technology as the iPhone 5s camera.
8. You can turn on most recent iPhone cameras by using the phone's +Volume button.	TRUE- This is probably the best way to take a picture without shaking the camera.
9. You can turn on most recent iPhone cameras by asking Siri to do it.	TRUE- But why would you want to do this?
10. The iPhone 6s has state-of-the-art 4K Video.	TRUE- Only a handful of other video and still cameras have 4K Video.

If you didn't score very high on our quiz, please don't feel badly. iPhone and iPad camera technology have evolved from a single, simple point-and-shoot camera into two highly sophisticated cameras— a forward-firing iSight camera that Apple calls the *rear camera*, and a backwards-facing FaceTime HD (*high-definition*) camera that Apple calls the *front camera*. Both have more advanced features than typical $300-$800 Japanese cameras.

However, the Japanese cameras usually come with 100-150 page PDF manuals. The iPhone doesn't come with a camera manual, and the camera chapter in the latest *Apple iPhone Users Guide* is only 6 pages long! Further, while Google, Yahoo and Amazon list many iPhone and iPad books, *The Compleat Apple iPhone and iPad Camera Guide* is one of the few camera manuals to include any information on how to use the many groundbreaking camera features introduced on the iPhone 6s and 6s Plus.

As one prominent writer who prefers to remain anonymous put it: *"Part of the Apple mystique is to provide one of the world's most sophisticated cameras ... but not a manual."*

It should take you no more than 1-2 hours to skim this book and learn dozens of things that will make you a more accomplished iPhone user. You will be amazed how much your photos will improve—and how much more you will do with your camera!

Introduction

An old professional photographer's adage is "The best camera is the one you have with you." Precisely because of this, the iPhone has become the world's most popular camera.

At the same time, the iPhone and iPad have evolved into some of the most advanced cameras you can buy for any price. Chapter 3 describes the unique features of the new iPhone 6s and 6s Plus, some of which few people have heard. Did you know that the iPhone 6s automatically records 1.5-second video clips before and after each photo? Did you know it can record in high-definition 4K Video, a technology that even some $2,000 video cameras don't use yet?

That's why I've written this book. It's only about 55 pages long, but it will allow you to make full use of your iPhone or Pad, regardless of which model you have. It will also give you lots of excuses for moving up to the newest models!

Above all, I hope you have a good time seeing what your iPhone and iPad cameras can do. I hope this book helps you approach these cameras with a spirit of wonderment - may the photos you create continually delight you.

One important note about my terminology: Apple refers to the camera that **fires toward other people** as the *rear camera*, since it is located on the backside of the iPhone or iPad. Similarly, they refer to the FaceTime HD camera which fires toward you as the *front camera*, since it is located on the front of the iPhone or iPad. This goes against all my instincts and training; a camera that fires toward others should be labeled as firing *frontwards*. However, I'll go along with Apple's terminology so as not to drive readers crazy when they go to their Apple manuals or call Apple's help lines.

CHAPTER ONE:
Twelve Features You NEED to Know

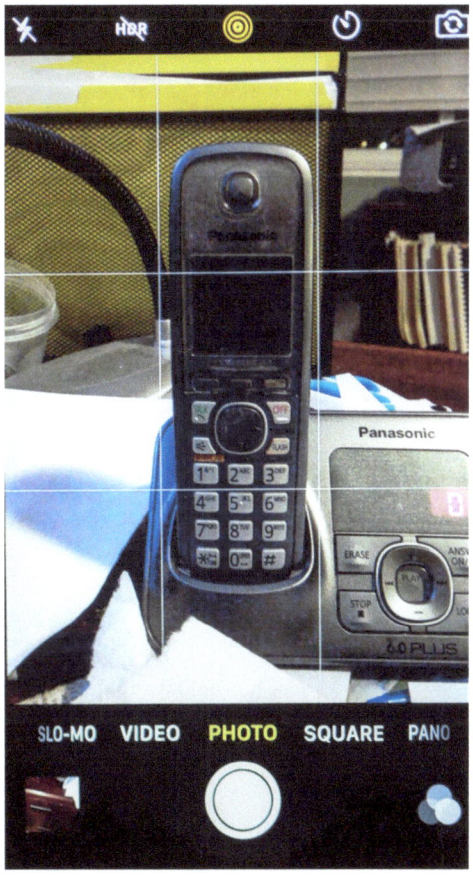

Opening Image

Overview

There are only 12 iPhone features you NEED to know to get good results from an iPhone or iPad camera:

- **Turning the Camera ON and OFF**

- **Composing the Picture**

- **Focusing the Cameras**

- **Taking Single and Burst Photos**

- **Taking Flash Photos**

- **Exposing the Image Properly**

- **"Zooming" In & Out**

- **Taking Selfies**

- **Selecting Photo Modes**

- **Taking Videos**

- **Reviewing Photos and Videos**

- **Uploading, Sharing, Editing, and Deleting Photos**

Turning the Camera ON and OFF

To turn your iPhone camera ON, tap the Camera icon on the main page. To turn the camera OFF, press the large recessed Home Button and the home screen will appear.

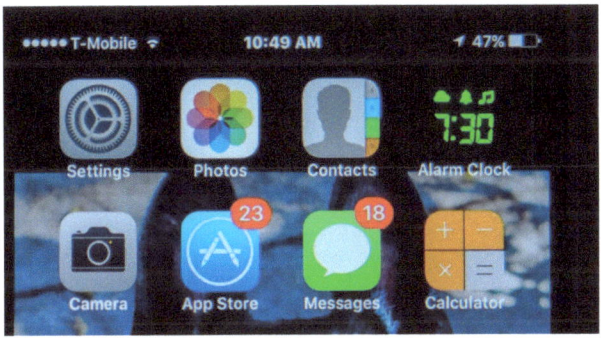

Camera Icon on my 6s Home Screen

Or, from the locked home screen, swipe up from the bottom edge of the screen to open the **Control Center** and then tap the camera icon in the lower-right corner.

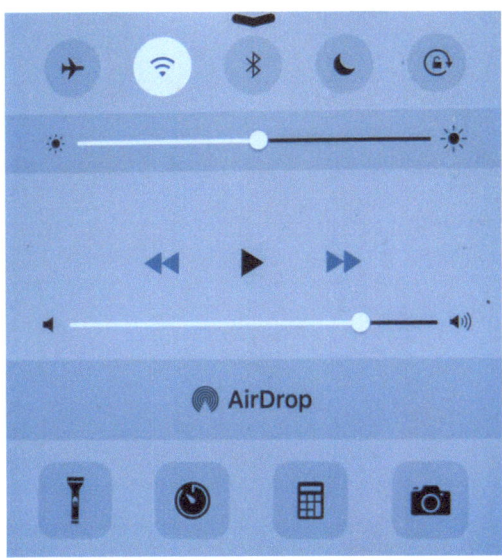

iPhone Control Center: Camera Icon on Lower Right

Composing the Picture

Once the camera is turned ON, point it at the subject or scene you wish to photograph. Providing there is not too much glare on the screen, just move the camera until the scene is exactly the one you wish to photograph. If glare is a problem, try shielding the screen with the hand that's not holding the iPhone or iPad. Try not to have your subject smack in the middle of the photo. Generally, the composition is more interesting if the subject if slightly off to the side and is involved in doing something, not just staring at the camera. But, as shown below, there are exceptions to every rule.

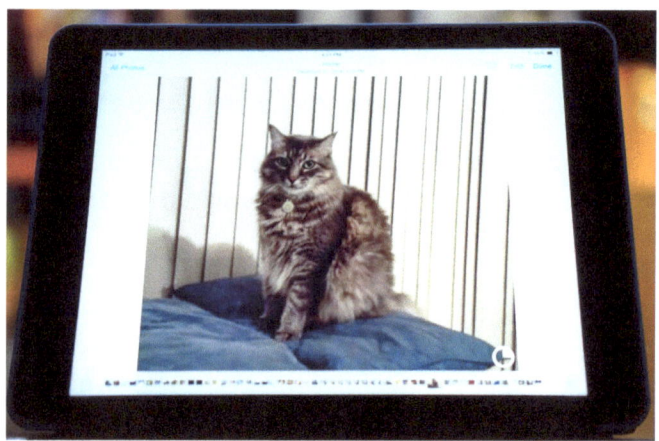

Photo On An iPad

Taking Single and Burst Photos

You take a single photo by lightly tapping the **large round white button** underneath the image. Tap it gently to take a single sharp photo.

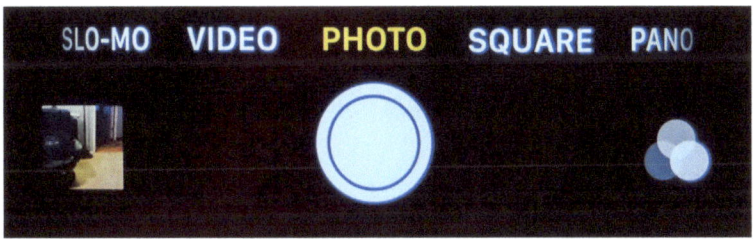

Shutter Button

Another way of activating the shutter is by pressing the **+Volume button** on the side of the iPhone. If you can get in the habit of firing the camera with the +Volume button, you'll be much less likely to produce a blurred image by moving the camera. This also works in Video Mode: pressing the **+Volume button** turns on the video and starts taking a movie, and pressing the **-Volume button** turns off the video camera.

If you hold the +Volume button down, or hold the large round white image of the shutter button on the camera screen down (rather than just tapping it), the camera will take repeated images at a rate of several frames per second. These are called **burst photos**. A counter will appear on the bottom half of the image showing how many photos you have taken.

Try to train yourself to shoot 3-shot bursts any time you are photographing kids, pets, sports activities, or when you're doing candid street shooting. Remember, the "film" is free in digital photography.

Taking Flash Photos

All the iPhones and iPads have an LED (*light-emitting diode*) light bulb built into them. This can be used as a flashlight or an alert (it can be set to flash when the phone rings, for instance). However, when the camera is on, the LED functions as an electronic flash.

You activate the flash mode by tapping the lightning icon in the top-left corner of the viewing screen. You'll then be given three choices: **AUTO**, **ON**, and **OFF**.

AUTO means that the flash will be activated only when the sensor needs the light.

ON means that the flash will fire every time. This can work well in a bright setting; the flash will provide fill-in light to smooth out the contrast in the scene, ensuring that no area is too light or too dark.

OFF means that the flash will never fire. This is the way many street shooters and serious photographers set their camera.

Starting with the iPhone 5s, the single white LED was replaced by two LEDs—one white and one amber—that fired simultaneously. The ratio of white-to-amber light was blended to optimize the color balance of the image. This makes the color balance of the photo look more natural.

Starting with the 6s, the white and amber light was blended to emit from a single LED. To the best of my knowledge, Apple's is the only flash that has this feature. Apple calls it True Tone Flash.

Focusing the Camera

iPhone cameras automatically focus themselves. Just point the camera toward your subject or scene, and the camera will come up with a pretty good guess of what area should be in sharp focus and which (if any) areas of the photo should be blurred.

Both the iSight front-firing camera and the FaceTime rear-firing camera have, in "camera-speak", *a fixed-length, 35mm-equivalent, fixed aperture f2.2 lens*. A 35-mm lens is considered a semi-wide angle lens; it keeps most objects in focus provided they're not very close to the camera.

However, unlike normal cameras, the f2.2 lens is unable to be stopped down to f4, f5.6 or f8 to increase the area that will be in focus, which is referred to in "camera-speak" as *depth of field*. This complicates the situation, since it means that unless the subjects of your photo are at least 10 feet away from the camera, the entire scene may not be in focus. The camera (or you) will have to decide what should be in focus. To decide what should be in the sharpest focus in a photograph, the iSight first looks to see if there are any faces in the scene. If so, the iSight will try to ensure that all the faces are in focus and are properly exposed. In "camera-speak" this is called *face recognition*.

A problem can occur if there are several strangers in a photo you are about to take, and you want your dog, who is sitting about 10 feet away from the strangers, to be the subject of the photo. In that case, as you compose the picture, tap the dog's image on the screen. A dotted box will appear around the dog's image, which will snap it into focus. You can then tap the shutter button or press the +Volume button to take the picture. The images of the strangers may be out of focus, but that's OK; the dog will be in focus, and that's what you wanted.

Exposing the Image Properly

As the camera automatically focuses on the image, it will also attempt to automatically expose the image so that it is neither too dark (*underexposed* in camera-speak) or too light (*overexposed* or *blown out* in camera-speak). First it will use face detection to properly expose faces, and then it will look at the overall scene to properly expose it.

However, to continue with the example in the previous section of how to focus on a dog standing apart from some strangers, when you tap on the dog's image to focus on the dog, and the dotted box appears around the dog, a slide control will also appear to the right of the dotted box. Moving the slide control upwards and downwards with your finger will adjust the exposure of the entire image so that you can make the dog the subject, not the strangers.

"Zooming" In & Out

There are quote marks around "zooming" because iPhones are not zoom cameras. Zoom cameras adjust their focal length from wide-angle to telephoto by moving the lens elements in and out.

There's no room to do this in iPhone cameras because they're too thin. Instead, iPhone cameras "zoom" by masking out part of the sensor; the zoomed-in image does not include the full area of the sensor. In "camera-speak" this is sometimes called *digital zoom* or *cropping*.

Digital zoom can be problematic when used too much. Any time an iPhone crops an image by only taking a part of it, it enlarges the pixels in the remaining portion of the image. This can damage the clarity and quality of your photos; use this feature very cautiously.

If you're trying to take a picture of a couple about 20 feet from the camera, point the iPhone towards them and—pressing your forefinger and thumb together—pinch over the part of the image that you want to enlarge and move your fingers slightly apart. The camera will zoom in on that part of the picture, and you'll get a zoomed-in image without having a zoom lens. To restore the image to its original form, place the thumb and forefinger about two inches apart on the screen and move them together as if you were pinching someone. This is a very useful feature if you use it in moderation.

A better technique is to walk closer to the subject! This will give you a better photo every time, and it's what professional photographers almost always do. Another option, which we will discuss in a later chapter, is to opt for a high-quality conventional camera to take high-quality telephoto images. Loyalty to your iPhone can only be carried so far!

Taking Selfies

Taking a *selfie* (slang for taking a photo of yourself or of any group that includes yourself) is accomplished by opening the camera application and then tapping on the **camera icon** in the upper-right corner of the screen. This activates the **FaceTime HD Camera**, the second camera that's hidden within your iSight camera. The FaceTime camera fires backwards so that you can take pictures of yourself.

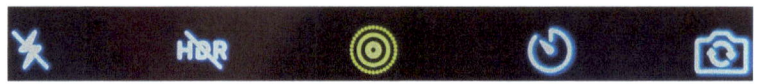

FaceTime Camera (Selfie) Icon Is On Far Right

The FaceTime camera, which is what we will call it from now on, has the same f2.2 aperture and 35mm focal length lens as the main iSight camera. It has a 5-megapixel sensor on the iPhone 6s and a 1.2-megapixel sensor on all other recent iPhone and iPads. Since most selfies are distributed via the Web, the FaceTime camera usually doesn't need the higher resolutions of the iSight camera.

When you take a selfie, you can also select flash mode, HDR mode, self-timer, photo format, video mode, and filters. When the flash mode fires with the FaceTime camera, the entire screen shines a bright white as the photo is taken. All the other controls (some of which we haven't discussed yet) work the same in the iSight and FaceTime modes.

Many photo enthusiasts who take a lot of selfies carry a selfie stick - an interesting new accessory. This is a small telescoping monopod with an iPhone bracket on one end and a handle on the other. Typically the handle end contains a button or trigger for firing the iPhone. In many tourist spots around the world, there are so many tourists waving these sticks in the air that there is serious consideration being given to banning them.

14

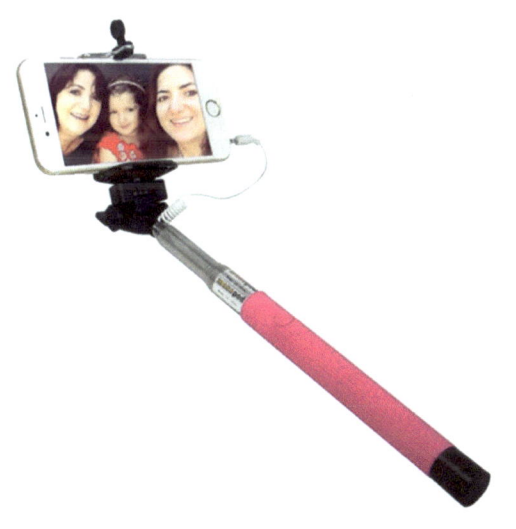

Selfie Stick

Selecting Photo Modes

The photo modes are listed across the screen just over the Shutter Button. They are:

- **Time Lapse** [hidden to the left on this screen]
- **Slo-Mo** (Slow Motion)
- **Video**
- **Photo**
- **Square**
- **Pano** (Panoramic)

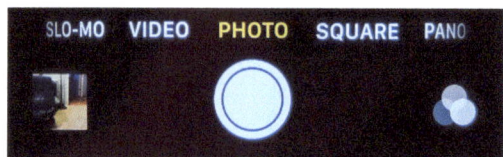

Photo Modes

Tap the photo mode you want, and the camera will stay in that mode—even if you turn the camera off—until another mode is selected. We'll discuss some of these modes in their own sections later on, but here is a concise description of what they do.

Time-Lapse: used to take photos of objects over a period to time to show how those objects move. Photos of the night sky taken every hour are an example. Time-lapse photos are typically assembled into video clips. The photos work best if the iPhone is mounted on a tripod or other kind of support.

Slo-Mo: slow-motion videos you might take of your buddy's golf swing to determine why he always slices to the left. They take pictures at a faster rate than regular videos, so that when the video is played back at a normal rate, you get a slow-motion effect.

Video: Video clips taken at normal speed.

Photo: Still photos taken in a rectangular format.

Square: Still photos taken in a square format.

Pano: Panoramic photos that encompass a much wider field of view than a normal photo.

Taking Videos

Taking videos is done fully automatically. Once you're in the Video Mode (Video Mode is the second choice under the shutter button), tap the large round shutter button to turn either the iSight or FaceTime camera ON, or do it with the +Volume Button on the left side of the iPhone.

Use the Camera Menu in Settings to choose between 30 or 60 frames per second (fps). 30 fps is the normal setting, and 60 fps is for taking high-definition videos. Personally, I'd opt for 60 fps in most instances.

Reviewing Photos and Videos

At the bottom-left corner of the screen, there is a small image of your last photo or video clip. Tap it, and it will appear full-size. If it's a video clip, tapping the large play button in the center will cause the video clip to play. If it's a photo, swipe from left to right with your thumb or any other finger and you will be able to review previous photos. Swipe from right to left and you will be able to review more recent photos.

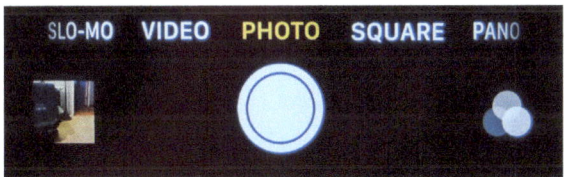

Enter Review Mode by Tapping Photo

Another way of reviewing your previous photos or video clips is to exit from the Camera app and tap the Photos icon. This is the easiest way to review any of your past photos. From here you can select those that you want to send out on social media and email, as well as decide which you want to store on your main PC or on iCloud.

Uploading, Sharing, Editing and Deleting

Overview

There are two ways to do activities such as Uploading, Sharing, Editing and Deleting. This book is written from the perspective of doing them via the **Camera Icon**, since the subject of this book is the iPhone's camera. However, the same functions can be accomplished in *very similar ways* through the iPhone's **Photo Icon**. This makes total sense if you think of the Camera icon as the iPhone's camera, and the Photo icon as the iPhone's filing system.

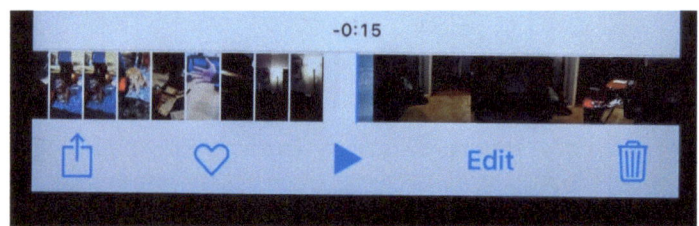

Uploading, Favorites, Play, Editing & Trash Controls

This section is written from the perspective of someone looking at the Camera section. What you will see if you look at the Photo section will be slightly different. The screen will also vary whether you are reviewing photos or videos. However, whether you're reviewing photos or videos, you will find 4-5 icons on this screen:

- Uploading
- Sharing
- Play (only there for videos)
- Editing
- Deleting

These are all **post-processing activities**. They take place after you have taken the photo or shot the video. This is sometimes confusing because some of them, such as filtering (a part of editing) can also take place while you are taking a photo.

For instance, for certain street shooting situations, you can decide in advance that you want to shoot in black and white because of the drama it can bring to the scene. In that case, you can use a black-and-white digital filter when you shoot the photos so that you have a good idea from the start how to compose and illuminate the photos. The iPhones offers three monochrome effects, which they call *Mono, Tonal,* and *Noir.* The alternative is to shoot the scene in color and then apply black-and-white filters in post-processing. If you choose to wait for post-processing, you can choose from Apple's three filters or from literally thousands of filters provided by outside vendors. Either option is OK. Most photographers will opt for selecting black and white filters in post-processing, but there are serious monochrome photographers who will spend $12,000 on a Leica Monochrome camera that can only shoot in black and white! These photographers see black and white photography as its own art form.

Uploading

Tapping the **Uploading** icon brings up a varying number of icons, depending on the applications that you have downloaded to your phone. My apologies if your list doesn't match mine.

The first row contains places to which you can upload a photo or a video. My list has:

- **Message**: Sends it as an instant message.
- **Mail**: Sends it within an e-mail.
- **iCloud Photo Sharing**: Sends it to your iCloud Photo Sharing site.
- **Notes**: Sends it to your Notes application.
- **Twitter**: Sends it to your Twitter account.
- **Facebook**: Sends it to your Facebook account.
- **Flickr**: Sends it to your Flickr account.
- **Save PDF to eBooks**: Saves it as a PDF in your eBooks account.

If there isn't room for all the icons to appear on the first line under the photo; tapping **MORE** will show you additional icons based on which apps you have installed on your iPhone.

A second line of **Actions** icons also appears under the photo. These are additional things you can do with the photo or video. Again, this list will vary depending on your downloads. My list has:

- **Copy**: Makes a duplicate photo or video.
- **Slideshow**: Converts your photos to a slide show, complete with music and a theme.
- **Hide**: Hides the photo or video from view, but does not delete it.
- **Assign to Contact**: Invaluable for salespeople; they can take a photo of everyone they meet and transfer the photo to the person's contact file.
- **Use as Wallpaper**: Use any photo as the background photo on your phone's home screen or lock screen.
- **Print:** If your iPhone is connected to a wireless printer, you can print photos directly from your phone.

Designating Favorites

Tap the Heart icon to designate those photos and videos that you want to ensure you cannot erase. If you change your mind, you can tap the Heart icon a second time to be able to erase it.

Editing

When you tap anywhere on the Editing Menu under a photo (including on the word "Edit" itself), you unleash a Pandora's Box of choices. It is better to upload a photo that you really care about to your laptop or PC and both catalog and edit it there, but Apple gives you the chance to do everything within the iPhone or iPad if you wish. Because of its larger screen size, the iPad is a much better choice for editing than the iPhone; I particularly recommend the new 12" iPad Pro. However, even that doesn't have the sophisticated editing software that's available for the MacBook Pro or a desktop unit.

Many iPhone users take photos with their iPhones, store them in the Cloud, and then transfer them to their iPad or MacBook Pro for editing before returning the edited images to the Cloud. This is the way to go if you have the hardware.

A confusing thing about the Edit menu is that it's nested. This means that every choice has lots of choices within it.

The first symbol is the **Crop Controls Icon**. Depending on which control you touch, you can reduce its vertical and horizontal size, tilt the image, change the overall dimensions of the image, or rotate the image. The best way to learn to use the crop commands is to try fooling around with them. You'll be amazed what they can do!

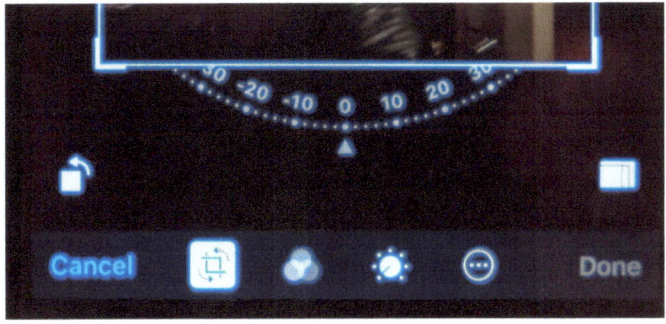

Cropping Controls

The second symbol is the **Filter Icon**. It applies eight different filters (None, Mono, Tonal, Noir, Fade, Chrome, Process, Transfer, Instant). I'd suggest that most of these are gimmicks—your most frequent choice should be **None**.

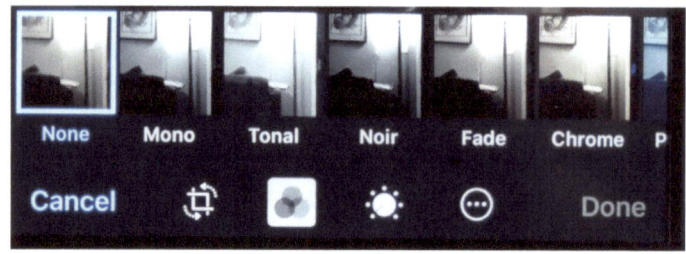

Filter Icons

The third symbol is the **Exposure Icon**. It brings up 3 submenus and 13 choices within them: Light (Exposure, Highlights, Shadows, Brightness, Contrast, Black Point); Color (Saturation, Contrast, Cast); B&W (Intensity, Neutrals, Tone, Grain). These choices can add impact to your photos, but they are much better applied when the photos have been transferred to a computer or iPad and edited with industry-standard software such as Adobe Lightroom.

The fourth symbol is the **External Programs Icon** that permits such programs as Camera+ to be used on the iPhone 6s. We will discuss these in a later chapter. This icon (a circle with 3 dots in it) is unique to the iPhone 6s.

The fifth Symbol is the word "**Done**"; tap this when you're done editing the photo.

Deleting

As on all iPhones and iPads, you delete a photo or video by tapping the **Trash Can Icon**. CAUTION: Deleting a photo removes it from the iCloud Photo Library and all your devices. In some cases it may be better to *Hide* a file (one of the Social Networking & Actions choices) rather than Delete it.

Magic Wand

In the upper right-hand corner of the edit screen, there is a magic wand symbol. You tap this if you think the camera can improve on the exposure and color balance of the photo, and the camera tries again. However, you can't give it any hints about what you want it to do; and since it has already set the exposure and color balance automatically, I'd suggest that you not get your hopes up too high that it will do better the second time. If you don't like the results, tap the wand again and it will go back to its original settings.

Magic Wand Icon (Live Photo Icon Is To the Left)

CHAPTER TWO:
Six Features That Are NICE to Know

Overview

There are six features of the iPhone cameras I'd classify as Nice to Know. These include:

- **Taking HDR Photos**
- **Using Built-in Filters While Taking a Photo**
- **Taking Panorama Photos**
- **Taking Slow-Motion Videos**
- **Tagging Locations**
- **Using the Settings/Photos & Camera Menu**

Don't be surprised if you don't know how to do more than a few of these things. Probably less than 10% of all iSight camera users know how to do all of them; and many probably don't know how to do a single one of them. A reason that you need this book is that most editions of the *Apple iPhone User Guides* devote less than one or two pages to these features!

Taking HDR Photos (HDR)

HDR photos are most frequently taken of landscapes. They are dramatic and have been described as *"3-D without the glasses."* A new generation of hi-definition TVs is on the horizon that will more fully exploit the capabilities of this technology. Also, the iPhone version of hi-definition can even be applied to selfies to create spectacular scenes of you and your significant other framed against a Hawaiian sunset.

HDR (High Dynamic Range) photos have only been able to be produced within cameras (as opposed to in PCs) for a few years. The idea originally was, if you encountered a landscape scene with a high dynamic range ("camera-speak" for a scene with very bright and dark sections within it), you could place the camera on a tripod and take several identical photos of the same scene that would be *bracketed*. That means that one image would be overexposed, one underexposed, and one correctly exposed. The three photos would then be superimposed on to one another by the computer software to form a much more dramatic single composite image than the original correctly-exposed photo.

Just recently, a few cameras have been engineered to replicate this function within the camera itself. The camera takes a burst of three bracketed photos (typically within a second) that have varied exposures, and the camera's firmware merges the three images into an HDR photo.

Starting with the iPhone 5s, Apple has joined this select group of HDR cameras. With a single click of the shutter, it fires off a burst of 3 shots and merges the photos into a single HDR image.

All of this takes place by tapping the HDR button on the screen. You can choose to have HDR be AUTO, ON or OFF. If you like the look of iPhone HDR photos (as I do), don't hesitate to keep the control on AUTO, in which case the camera decides when it should be used. HDR can be activated for both the iSight forward-firing camera and for the FaceTime HD rear-firing camera.

HDR is found on the Top Camera menu. In the following screen shot, HDR was turned off.

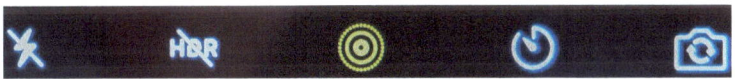

Top Camera Menu with HDR and Flash OFF and Live Photos activated

Immediately after tapping HDR, this appeared:

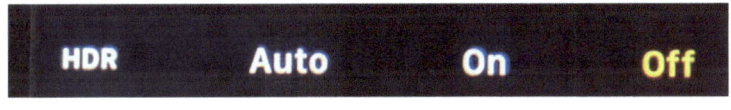

HDR Sub-Menu

If you become a devotee of HDR photography, there are some third-party software programs that, usually for $1.99 each, will provide you with an even-better HDR function. We'll discuss two of these in a later chapter.

One of the Photo and Camera menu settings that we'll discuss later in this chapter permits you to save both the HDR and the regular versions of a photo. Be sure to keep this control ON so you will always have the option of choosing which version of your photo you will use.

HDR, along with 4K Video, is practically unknown now because so few high-definition TVs can do justice to either one. But according to *The Wall Street Journal,* starting with the 2015 Christmas buying season, HDR TVs will be one of the hottest luxury items. These televisions can display HDR videos and photos as well as 4K videos. On November 11, 2015, Geoffrey Fowler called HDR TVs *"the best argument in years to upgrade your set."* As HDR TVs become mainstream, HDR photos and 4K photos will become mainstays of iPhone photography.

In the meantime, start fooling around with this feature. It is truly one of the high points of iPhone and iPad photography; and it can dramatically improve your travel photos.

Using Built-In Filters

If you press the **Three-Circles Icon** in the lower right-hand corner of the screen, nine different variants of your image will appear on the screen:

- **Mono**
- **Tonal**
- **Noir**
- **Fade**
- **None** (No Filter)
- **Chrome**
- **Process**
- **Transfer**
- **Instant**

Rather than try to explain what these filters do, I'll suggest that you simply try them out by tapping each one of them yourself.

My suggestion is that you should stay away from using the built-in digital filters most of the time. You are much better off setting the filter to **None** and then applying a filter as a part of post-processing. If you are using one of the popular post-processing software packages such as *Adobe Lightroom*, you can buy literally dozens of truly high-quality filters for just a few dollars. In fact you can buy filters that can emulate all of the famous color and black-and-white film emulsions such as Tri-X, Plus-X, and Kodachrome. You can also purchase filter-like software to smooth out skin or hide a double chin.

When you're taking photos, concentrate on composition, exposure, and emotion; leave the gimmicks until it's late at night and you're experimenting on your computer.

Taking Panoramic Photos (PANA)

Taking panoramic photos usually involves mounting your camera on a tripod and taking overlapping photos of a 180-degree panorama at a scenic location. The camera then stitches these images together into a single photo, making it look like it was taken by an ultra-wide angle lens. Like HDR photos and digitally filtered photos, panoramic photos are ones you either love or hate. They are an acquired taste, and few people are neutral about them.

It's difficult to make high-quality panoramic photos without having the iPhone mounted on a tripod or a flat surface on which you can rotate the camera. To take this type of photograph, select the Pano mode, press the shutter button, and pan the camera ("camera-speak" for moving it slowly and evenly) in the direction of the arrow. You can pan either horizontally (the usual case for scenic panoramas) or vertically (for a panoramic view of the Empire State Building or a waterfall). When you're done panning, press the shutter button a second time to shut the camera off. You can only pan the iSight camera, and you can only make these images in Photo mode; it doesn't work with selfies, and it doesn't work with HDR.

The resulting photo will be long and narrow—almost like a strip of film. However, unlike a film strip or a video, the image is not divided into a series of discrete photos. It is a single photo that has been stitched together.

Taking Slow-Motion Videos (SLO-MO)

There's no difference between taking regular videos and **SLO-MO videos** except that with SLO-MO, you're taking many more frames each second. When you play back a SLO-MO video, rapid motions are slowed down and smoothed out. Slow-motion photography can be used to analyze the way you swing a golf club or the way your child swings his or her bat in softball. It's also good for dramatic scenes of people running towards each other, or for science fair projects in which your child figures out how hummingbirds fly.

To use Slow Motion mode, tap the word SLO-MO and then tap the shutter button on the screen or press the +Volume control on the iPhone. Press a second time to end the video clip.

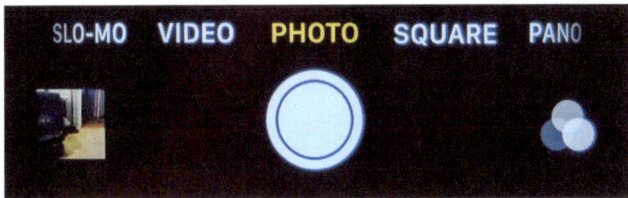

SLO-MO

Using the Settings/PHOTOS & CAMERA Menu

There are several **PHOTOS & CAMERA** menu preferences that can be turned ON and OFF by first tapping the Settings Icon on the Home Screen and then tapping the "Photos & Camera" menu item that appears pretty far down the list of settings.

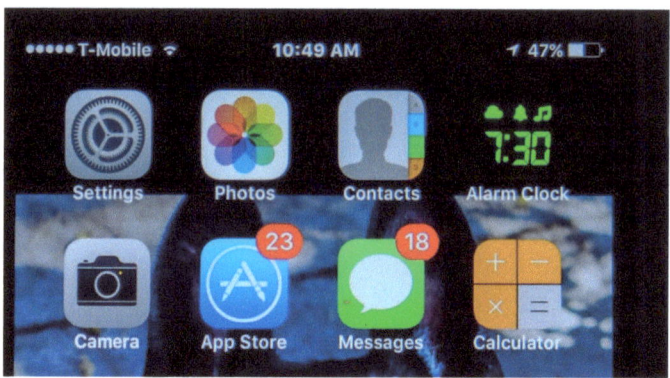

Home Screen's Photos and Camera Icons

To understand the Photos & Camera Menu, you will need to understand what the Photos Icon and the Camera Icon do. You already understand the Camera Icon, so here is a brief explanation of the Photos App.

Photos (iPhoto)

Photos (or iPhoto) is a library that contains every photo and video stored in your iPhone or iPad. Think of it as a filing cabinet on steroids. It can **upload** to all the places to which your iPhone camera can upload; it can mark any photo or video you select as a **favorite**; and it can **delete** any photo or video you select. Also, it can **edit** any photo you select using the same edit commands that you have learned within the Camera App.

Its real power is how it can interface with the iCloud Photo Library that stores all the photos you've ever taken on any device. In my case, this means that while I'm sailing on a ship in the

Mediterranean this spring, I'm able to download photos to my iPad that I shot at home 6 years before.

The Photo Stream is the set of photos that is sent to every one of my Apple devices every time I sign onto the Cloud, thus assuring that every device has an updated complete set of all my photos.

Photos & Camera Settings That Affect iPhone, iPad and iCloud Storage

Here's a brief explanation of these storage options. My preferred setting follows in parentheses.

iCloud Photo Library (On/Off): Automatically uploads all photos and videos to the cloud (**ON**).

Download & Keep Originals (On/Off): When I'm connected to Wi-Fi, my originals are sent to the cloud and small copies are stored on my devices (**ON**).

Upload to My Photo Stream (On/Off): My photos are sent to all my devices (**ON**).

Upload Burst Photos (Yes/No): All burst photos are sent to my Photo Stream (**YES**).

iCloud Photo Sharing (Yes/No): Creates albums to share with other people and subscribes to other people's albums (**NO**).

Summarize Photos (Yes/No): Summarizes your photos by Collections and Years (**YES**).

Grid: Turning this feature ON will help you compose your image by dividing it into a 3x3 grid. It also helps ensure that the images will be level and vertical. Using it is strictly a matter of taste. Try it and see if you like it.

Record Video: If you have the iPhone 6s, I recommend selecting **4K at 30 fps**. This creates stunning, state-of-the-art videos that only a few DSLRs and mirrorless cameras can match. If you have an older iPhone, I recommend selecting **1080HD at 60 fps**.

Record Slo-Mo: Select the fastest setting, **1080 HD at 240 fps**. The additional recording space this will require is worth the additional resolution you will gain.

HDR (High Dynamic Range): "Keep Normal Photo" should always be **ON**. This will save the HDR and the normal copy of all your photos.

I should note that I tend to select settings that use the most memory because they also produce the highest quality photos. One reason that I can do this is that I only use my iPhone for photography, telephone calls, and reading books. I do not use my phone for listening to music or watching videos. Also, I always tend to buy the largest memory iPhone available at the time they are released. If you buy smaller iPhones or if you use them for a wider variety of purposes, you may not be able to follow my recommendations since you can't add extra storage devices to iPhones and iPads.

Tagging Locations

Tagging Locations allows iPhones to automatically identify the GPS (global positioning) coordinates of where a photo was taken. Once the GPS coordinates are known, iCloud automatically identifies a photo of a painting as having been taken in the at a museum in San Francisco 6 years earlier.

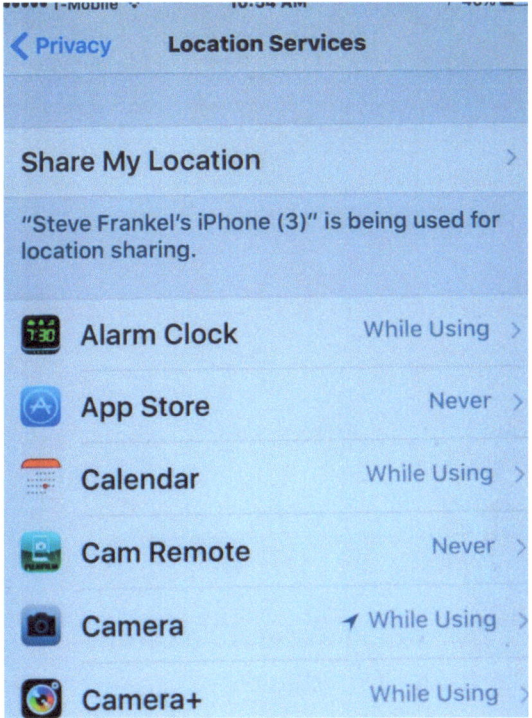

Location Services Menu

This magic is accomplished with a setting that's hidden in the **Privacy Menu** that you get to via the **Settings Icon**. It's in the menu group called **Location Services**. Be sure all the Location Services listed under **Photos & Camera** are turned ON. This permits the GPS coordinates of all your photos to be recorded when you take a photo. Twenty years from now, when you've taken photos of your kids at amusement parks all over the country, you'll thank me for this advice.

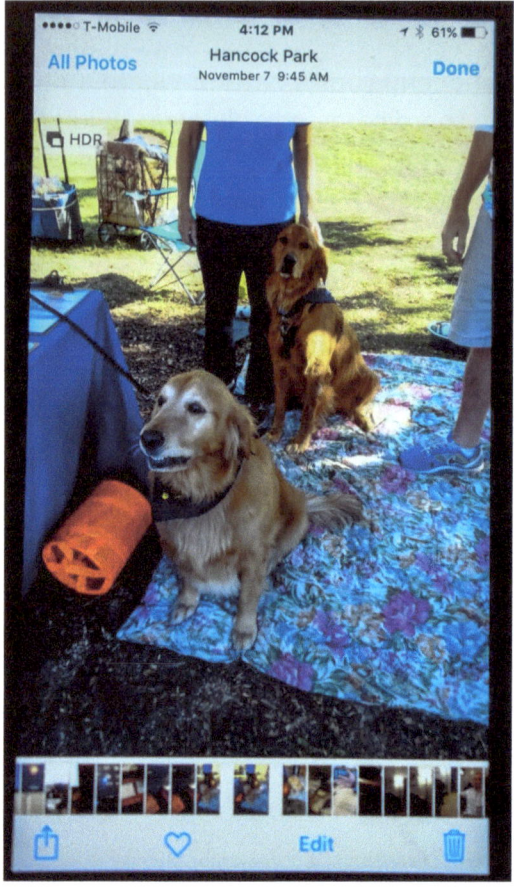

iCloud Knows This Was Taken in Hancock Park

The GPS coordinates are part of a photo's *metadata* that's hidden within each photo. iCloud reads this metadata and converts it into the name of the location.

CHAPTER THREE:
Features Found Only on the iPhoto 6s and 6s Plus

Apple's Upgrading Strategy

Most of the new iPhone features are introduced when Apple makes major model changes - about every two years - such as the move from the iPhone 5 to the iPhone 6. Apple uses these major changeovers to improve many things about the iPhones, but not necessarily the iPhone or iPad cameras.

Instead, the big changes for the cameras are introduced during the "off-years," such as when Apple changed from the iPhone 6 to the 6s. These "s year" transformations also happen every two years, since a typical progression for Apple is:

    2015 - Apple 6s
    2014 - Apple 6
    2013 - Apple 5s
    2012 - Apple 5

It is significant that the iPad has never had a significant camera upgrade. All the newest ones, including the new 12" iPad Pro, are using variants of the iPhone 5s camera.

Just to confuse things even more, in 2014 Apple added the Apple 6 Plus and in 2015 it added the Apple 6s Plus. Plus models are known solely for their larger size, but Apple added some improvements to these phones that were not shared with the smaller models.

As this is being written in early November 2015, some of the iPhone 6s and iPhone 6s Plus camera features have just been introduced. Here is what we know regarding the 6s and the 6s Plus camera improvements.

iSight 12-Megapixel Sensor and FaceTime 5-Megapixel Sensor

The main iSight forward-firing camera sensor has been improved from 8 megapixels to 12 megapixels. This is truly a big deal because it makes the iPhone's camera sensor about comparable in size and memory capacity to some of the Japanese small-sensor point-and-shoot cameras. In turn, these Japanese cameras are being driven closer to the point of extinction by the iPhones and Android smartphones.

The only small-sensor point-and-shoot cameras that still make sense today are those that have a high-quality zoom lenses/or a great viewfinder. Otherwise, for casual use, all you need is your smartphone.

Similarly, the rear-firing FaceTime Sensor was increased from 1.2 megapixels to 5 megapixels. This makes it possible to make 8" x 10" prints of your selfies to display on desks or "brag walls."

From a marketing standpoint, this was a canny move on Apple's part. Every photo and video taken with a 6s will require more memory capacity, and this means that many larger-memory models will be sold at premium prices.

Live Photos

A new feature called **Live Photos** automatically captures 1.5 seconds of video immediately before and after you take a photo. These images can be taken with either the main iSight camera or with the rear-firing FaceTime camera. If the concentric-circle icon above the image is lit, video clips will be created for every photo until you turn the feature off. To see the video clips, just press down a little harder than usual after you select photos to review. Apple calls this **3-D Touch**. Often the video clip will be more interesting than the photo itself!

This new feature promises to be a game-changer. To the best of my knowledge, it's not yet possible to access the video clips to produce additional still images, but it's only a matter of time until Apple or a third party comes out with an application to do this. Other upgrades could potentially lengthen the periods during which the clips are recorded.

Retina Flash

Retina Flash is a pre-flash, much like studio photographers use with a light box, to preview and adjust the effects of light on a subject. It's only used with the FaceTime camera. When the selfie is taken, the whole screen lights up, the sensor judges the effects of the light, and the camera adjusts the light while the photo is taken.

The idea is to produce high-quality indoor selfies without requiring any more skill by the photographers. Combine this with the new 5-megapixel FaceTime sensor, and selfies are no longer a teenage fad!

High Def 4K Video

To go along with the HDR (High Dynamic Range) capability that Apple added two years ago with the iPhone 5s, Apple has added **High Def 4K Video** to iPhone 6s. This high-end feature is just now appearing on larger cameras that typically cost more than $1,000 for the body and a quality lens.

As noted in the last chapter, 4K Video is turned on via the **Settings Icon** and the **Photos & Camera** menu. When 4K Video is turned on, a notation appears on the camera screen when video recording is selected. When you press the ON button to start recording, the ON button switches to a square shape to signify it's now an OFF button. A second, smaller round ON button also appears; if you press this while you are making a 4K video, you get an 8K photo! You can press the button as many times as you want; each time you will be taking an 8K still photograph. This gives you the best of both worlds for shooting action photos: movie clips plus still photos.

This high-definition film option is ideal for shooting folk dancing, for instance. You can take a video of the overall dancing, but shoot still photos of the dancers' expressions.

Another neat feature of 4K video shooting is that it permits 3X digital zoom by widening your fingers. While photographing a group of dancers, you can zoom in on one who is particularly photogenic.

Optical Image Stabilization (OIS)

The **iPhone 6s Plus** now has a true Optical Image Stabilization (OIS) feature. Sometimes called anti-shake, this comes in handy when you're taking low-light shots without a flash. It senses the movements of the camera and compensates with tiny movements of the lens to keep the camera steady. Some cameras and lenses, such as those made by Fujifilm, actually have tiny gyroscopes built into them to compensate for movements by the person taking the photo.

The product announcement for the iPhone 6s Plus says that it includes true OIS. The 5s, 6, and 6s emulate OIS digitally (as several inexpensive regular cameras do), but it really must have been a challenge for Apple to have installed a mechanical OIS into the 6s Plus. A web search reveals that the 6s Plus indeed has true OIS, and it's particularly effective with 4K Video. There are several videos online comparing a 6s 4K video with digital stabilization with a 6s Plus 4K video with OIS stabilization. The differences are marked. However, only one article says how Apple does it—it suggests that it too uses a gyroscope system but gives no details.

Higher-Resolving Screen and Improved Processing Engine

The **iPhone 6s Plus** has a higher-resolving screen (**1334 x 750** vs. **1136 x 640** pixel images) than other recent iPhones, including the 6s. There are several other differences between the 6s and 6s Plus as well.

My wife, Jill, "inherited" my iPhone 6 when I bought my iPhone 6s Plus, and so I have had ample opportunities to see and use them side-by-side. From a photographic standpoint, there is no comparison: the 6s Plus camera is dramatically better in every way.

Apple knows exactly what it is doing in providing camera improvements in the "off-year" models. They are trying to get photo enthusiasts to trade-up their phones every year: one year you trade to get the phone's features, and the other year you trade to get the camera's features. Go with it.

If you're a photo enthusiast, run don't walk to your Apple provider and trade in your present iPhone 5s or 6 for the iPhone 6s Plus. That's the only model that true *gear heads* ("camera-speak" for someone who always wants to have the latest-and-greatest camera) should consider at this time.

Luckily, the phone carriers such as Verizon and T-Mobile are falling into line with this strategy. Several of them are permitting annual trade-ins for a $5/month premium. At this point – especially if you're a gear head – it's well worth it.

CHAPTER FOUR:
Software Apps Worth Downloading

Third-Party Software Worth Downloading

Apple has always been known for compiling a huge collection of third-party software applications that sell in the iTunes Store, sometimes called the App Store, for a few dollars each. By not limiting software development (and the production of product-related books and media) to Apple's internal staff, true innovations occur as independent developers and writers sense opportunities to add products to the Apple pipeline.

There are three kinds of Apple software I'd recommend that you purchase. Considering that a "bundle" of all three software types can cost less than $10, these ought to be painless purchases":

- **Exposure Control Software**
- **Advanced HDR Software**
- **Social Networking Software**

One of the underlying principles of Apple software development is not to provide users with features that are difficult to use. This is why iSight cameras don't permit full manual control of features such as lens aperture and shutter speeds—and it's also why large sets of digital filters are not provided. However, enough iPhone users are experienced photographers that these are economically feasible add-ons for third-party developers. While we haven't tested them, application programs such as *Camera+* and *ProCamera + HDR, Photo Editing, Custom Filters, Effects and Video* are worth considering at $1.99 and $4.99 respectively.

Apple is just getting into HDR photography, and their latest effort in the iPhone 5s again trades off manual control for ease-of-use. If you want to experiment with this ground-breaking function which can make so many mundane photos sparkle, consider investing $1.99 in a program such as *Simply HDR* or the *HDR, Photo Editing, Custom Filters, Effects and Video* software mentioned earlier. They give you much more control over the HDR functions and allow you to experiment with the variables that go into implementing this effect.

There are some wildly popular social networking sites that you might want to download that encourage photographs along with other media. Most are free, or have free versions. These include iCloud, Flickr, LinkedIn, Twitter, Instagram, and Facebook.

There are also sites that are specifically aimed at photographers who want to sell or show off their work. These include 500px, Photobucket, Shutterfly, and SmugMug. These apps all have international followings measured in the millions of users, and most have both free and paid versions.

The book *The Art of iPhone Photography* by Bob Weil and Nicki Fitz-Gerald (Rocky Nook, Inc., 2013) provides a fantastic introduction to third-party software for the iPhone. It is sometimes available in eBook format for a little as $9.95. It is a compilation of phenomenal photographs taken by a dozen photographers who each describe how they used more than 60 different iPhone software packages (including all those I've mentioned above) to create their images. I'd consider this essential reading for anyone interested in going further with their iPhone photography.

Post-Processing Software

Finally, every photo enthusiast should have a post-processing program on his or her laptop or desktop that they can use both to organize their photos and to edit them. You will be able to edit more extensively and with better results on a computer than with either an iPhone or iPad program. The leader in this category is *Adobe Lightroom*, but it generally costs more than $100 a year to use.

There are many other programs in this category as well. However, these are *use it or lose it programs.* This means unless you use it regularly, you soon lose touch with how to use it effectively. Therefore, at this point, since I've been using Lightroom exclusively for the past five years, I leave it to others to recommend alternatives.

CHAPTER FIVE:
iPad Photography

Photo Activities At Which iPads Excel

iPads excel at sharing and displaying photos taken with other devices, especially iPhones. Your iPhone photos can be downloaded from My Photo Stream and the iCloud Photo Library on to your iPad. The iPad is great for sharing many images with individuals, and you can organize your photos into slide shows that can be edited and organized. When you do this, the iPhone photos are geomapped and their locations are added to the photos' metadata.

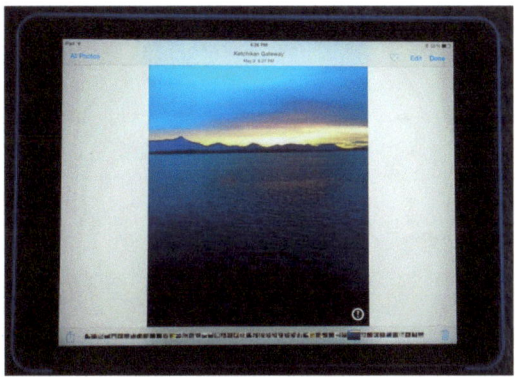

No iPhone Can Match This Screen!

Because of the increased performance and portability of iPhones, many people who own iPads also own iPhones that they rely upon as their primary cameras. However, many use their iPads as a storage device to save their favorite photos and as a viewing device to show them off. When they are somewhere where they don't wish to carry a cell phone (such in a foreign country or onboard a cruise ship), they may use the iPad as their primary camera and primary email device. Yet most of the time, photographic uses are secondary. iPads are usually used to view TV shows and movies, surf the web, and handle email, as well as interact with social media.

Difference Between Models

The iPad cameras are a generation behind iPhones. The latest iPads are the **iPad Air 2** and the **iPad Pro.** These two models (and the iPad Air that came before them) have the same cameras and features that are in the iPhoto 5s. They all contend with some challenges that we will discuss below, but their screens put the iPhone 6s to shame in terms of their size and impact.

- **The iPad Air** had a 5-MP (mega-pixel) processor for the main camera and a 1.2-MP for the FaceTime processor. Its speed and resolution is slightly inferior to the iPad Air 2. My wife uses her iPad Air every day, and other than slightly poorer resolution and reduced Wi-Fi performance compared to my iPad Air 2, it works very well.

- **The iPad Air 2** has an 8-MP processor for the main camera and a 1.2-MP processor for the FaceTime camera. Its speed and Wi-Fi performance is about equal to that of the iPhone 5s with which it shares an engine. It has a great display and terrific performance.

- **The iPad Pro** has the same processing engine and camera as the iPad Air 2, and a spectacularly larger, brighter and higher resolving screen. As I write this, it has only been on the market for one day! I will update this section when I get the chance to use the camera.

Challenges With iPad Photography

iPad cameras look and act the same as their iPhone counterparts. If you can work one, you can work the other. However, there are several challenges that iPad photo enthusiasts must contend with:

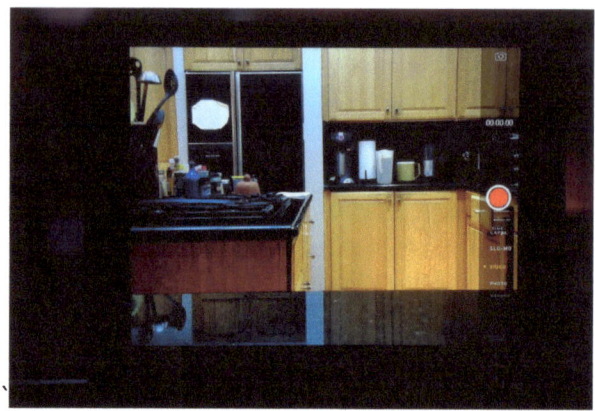

iPad Camera Screen

Glare: Increasing numbers of people enjoy using iPads as cameras when they are indoors, but they sometimes encounter problems using them outdoors in the bright sun because of glare on the screen. Hopefully, Apple is working on glare-free glass for iPads that will solve this problem in the next few years. In the next section, we'll discuss some ways of addressing this problem.

Grips: It's only a matter of time before someone makes millions patenting a small, handy (no pun intended) grip for the iPad that will do for iPads what the selfie stick did for iPhones. iPads can be hard to hold onto; especially when you're on the bow of a rolling ship or trying to get a shot of your kid marching in the St. Patrick's Day Parade.

Optical Image Stabilization (OIS): OIS helps keep a camera steady when you are trying to get an available light photo of a harbor by moonlight. OIS is already available on the iPhone 6s Plus, so it's hopefully coming to iPads some time in the future.

It is likely that all of these problems will be solved by Apple and other companies within the next 2-3 years. For all we know, Apple is on the verge of releasing an "s" model this spring that will address all of these issues; and the Apple Store, Amazon, and eBay will have dozens of offerings addressing these same issues.

In the meantime, I don't go anywhere I want to show my photos without my iPad. I also sometimes use it to share chapters of the books I'm writing. If a photo opportunity comes up when I'm using it for one of these activities, I happily take advantage of its availability to use it as a camera; if it's more convenient to use than my iPhone 6s or one of my "real cameras."

CHAPTER SIX:
When Only a "Real Camera" Will Do

Overview

iPhones and iPads have come a long way in the past five years, especially when it comes to being able to replace "real cameras" such as those made by Canon, Nikon, Fujifilm, Ricoh, Sony, Panasonic, Olympus and Leica.

Although some professionals and gifted amateurs are not eager to admit it, nearly all use smartphones at least occasionally when they in the field and larger cameras are not immediately available. Many photographers advise people to use smartphones when street shooting, since with smartphones it's hard to determine when you're just talking on the phone or taking a candid photo. This makes them highly useful for shooting candid photos in dicey situations, such as during political demonstrations or in drinking establishments.

Nevertheless, there are some times when, as of now, you will need a traditional camera.

There are three main limitations to using iPhone cameras that have yet to be overcome:

- Lack of telephoto capabilities
- Small sensor size
- Lack of a viewfinder

Lack of Telephoto Capabilities

No matter how much you love your iPhone or iPad, if you sign up on for a cruise to Patagonia or Antarctica where the greatest reward for your $10,000, two-week investment is spending a few hours one day photographing penguins from a blind 40-50 feet away, your iPhone or iPad will be completely useless. For that kind of shooting situation—unless you already have and know how to use pro-level equipment—I favor lightweight super-zoom cameras such as the $600 28-300mm f2.8 constant aperture Olympus Stylus 1s, or the $400 25-600mm constant aperture f2.8 Lumix FZ-200. Weighing under a pound apiece, their wide-range zooms, fast apertures, electronic viewfinders and sharp lenses make them ideal for wildlife and travel photography if you are not looking to mount huge prints on your walls.

I've used both of these cameras on extended cruses for several weeks at a time. My personal favorite is the Olympus Stylus 1s, because it has one of the best electronic viewfinders (EVFs) available today. I used it as my principal camera on a three-week cruise to Japan, Siberia and Alaska and it produced 1,600 beautiful photos without a single malfunction. While it's not pocket-szed, it only weighs 14 ounces; meaning that – paired with an iPhone 6s Plus – it doesn't weigh much more than a pound. My book, *The Compleat Olympus Stylus 1s (*available from Amazon in Kindle and paperback format*)*, has more than 20 full-page color photos taken with this camera. These are particularly impressive in the paperback version.

However, if you encounter situations where you would normally need a telephoto lens and you only have your iPhone, don't despair ...GET CLOSER! Zoom with your feet! Overcome your normal reluctance to get in someone's face and get the shot! This is an old newsman's trick, and you will be surprised how effective it is.

Small Sensor Size

While most of my photos these days end up on the web, I have dedicated a certain amount of wall space in my home to the photo efforts of which I'm the most proud. The framed photos that go in these spaces are mostly printed on canvas or paper; they are 13" x 19", 16" x 20", 24" x 24" and 20" x 24" in size.

Because the iPhone and iPad sensor is so small (about the size of a man's thumbnail), it is virtually impossible to get a high-quality enlargement from an iPhone or iPad.

This is a case where *"size matters."* I always keep several "real cameras" of varying sizes that I use in situations where I think there is a good chance that I will want to create high-quality prints.

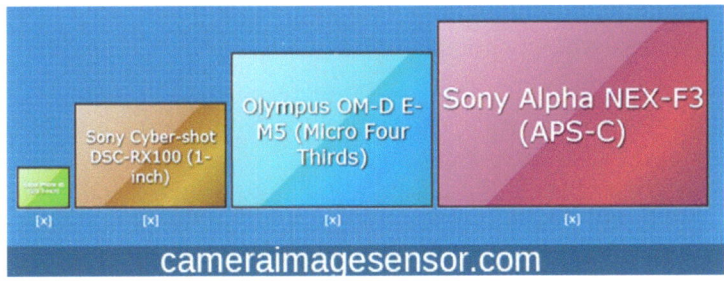

Relative Sensor Sizes (from Cameraimagesensor.com)

This is a comparison chart provided by cameraimagesensor.com. The green image is an iPhone sensor, full-size. Coincidently, the brown image is my favorite pocket camera, the Sony RX100, which I use in place of the iPhone when I want framed prints from a pocket camera that the iPhone can't make. The difference in the size of the sensors explains why the Sony RX100 can make a beautiful 13" x 19" print and the iPhone can't.

The aqua image is the Micro Four Thirds sensor that some Olympus and Panasonic/Lumix cameras use. It's generally regarded as the smallest sensor capable of professional-quality work. I've used the Olympus OM-D line of cameras for more than 10,000 travel photos and have seldom been disappointed. Looking at the diagram, the Micro-Four Thirds sensor appears to be about 25 times larger than iPhone sensor.

The red image represents the APS-C sensor that Sony, Fujifilm, Nikon and Canon rely on for their workhorse cameras. I presently use a Fujifilm T-X1 with two zoom lenses and one fixed-length lens. The camera and two of the lenses are weatherproof, and everything—including a small camera bag— weighs less than 5 pounds. This pro-level setup costs about $2,700; but it can produce high-quality travel and street photos anywhere I take it.

If I needed to produce the highest-quality work with an iPhone or iPad, I would look to shoot where I had ample lighting and subjects that were stationary or moved slowly. I would also look to shoot photos that were high in human interest and evoked emotions, since that causes people to overlook the technical aspects of a photo and focus instead on the photo's message.

Lack of a Viewfinder

For my styles of travel and street photography, the cameras I use have to have electronic viewfinders (EVFs) with eyecups that shield them from glare. An EVF is another candidate for an accessory or upgrade for a future iPhone or iPad, but until then it makes reliance on "real cameras" a necessity for many photographers when shooting outdoors.

Among relatively inexpensive cameras, the EVF on the Olympus Stylus 1s is the best I've ever seen. On more expensive cameras, I favor the EVFs on the Fujifilm X-T1 and the Olympus OM-D-M5. All of these EVFs require rubber eyecups to provide their best performance.

However, if I were shooting in a place and time that demanded a viewfinder and all I had was my iPhone or iPad, I would do my best to shield the screen with my hand or my body, or even set up something or somebody to shield me from the sun when I was taking photos. Don't worry about looking peculiar for a few moments; it's getting the shot that counts!

CHAPTER SEVEN:
HELP!!!

This is an easy chapter to write. If you've gone to the expense of purchasing an iPhone or iPad, it deserves a 2-year AppleCare+ contract which will set you back $99 and even covers water damage and accidental breakage for a fee of $79 for iPhones and $99 for iPads. Other than those problems, AppleCare will virtually always take care of whatever ails you for no cost. The telephone support is terrific, and the carry-in support is equally good—particularly if you have an appointment at the Genius Bar.

Remember, your iPhone comes with a 15-day return policy and 90 days of free Apple Care support. If you don't want to spring for Apple Care, your teenage relatives are probably your best alternative—followed by Googling the problem online.

Acknowledgements

It's not easy to live with a stay-at-home writer who spends 12 hours a day at his computer and much of the rest of the time playing around with the devices he's writing about. Thank you Jill for your patience and understanding, and for all you do to take up the slack. And thank you, Shadow and Sailor (who has just passed over the Rainbow Bridge), for your willingness to rearrange your play times, feeding times, and sleeping times around my writing.

The Author

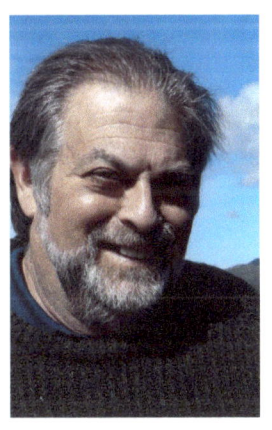

Steve Frankel is an avid travel photographer and street shooter who has logged about 200,000 miles on cruise ships with his wife Jill; and shot more than 40,000 photos in the past 15 years. He is an avid gear head with a compulsion for always trying out the newest cameras. According to his *Lightroom* catalogs, he has used more than 50 different cameras and 100 lenses during the past decade. When he photographs in Los Angeles, his shooting companion is often Shadow, a 95-pound black German shepherd who walks quietly alongside him and greets his subjects with a friendly smile.

Steve is the senior author and publisher of The Compleat Press (www.TheCompleatPress.com). He is the author of *The Compleat Olympus Stylus 1s, The Compleat Olympus Tough TG-4 and TG-850 Camera*, and *The Compleat iPhone & iPad Camera Guide. The Compleat Android Camera Guide* and a new series, *The Compleat Photo Traveler,* will follow this book in 2016.

Steve lives in Playa del Rey, California. He formerly lived in the Washington DC area where he was a Contributing Editor of *The Washingonian Magazine,* a member of The National Press Club and the author of several best-selling computer books.

IF YOU ENJOYED THIS BOOK, PLEASE GIVE US A **LIKE** AT OUR FACEBOOK SITE, www.Facebook.com/TheCompleatPress, WHERE YOU'RE ALSO INVITED TO CONTRIBUTE YOUR FAVORITE iPHONE AND iPAD PHOTOS; AND PLEASE REGISTER AT OUR WEBSITE, www.TheCompleatPress.com FOR FREE UPDATES AND NEWS OF UPCOMING EVENTS AND BOOKS.

www.ingramcontent.com/pod-product-compliance
Lightning Source LLC
Chambersburg PA
CBHW041106180526
45172CB00001B/126